AN IMAGINATION LIBRARY SERIES

Colors of the Sea

CORAL REEF BUILDERS

Eric Ethan and Marie Bearanger

Gareth Stevens Publishing
MILWAUKEE

For a free color catalog describing Gareth Stevens Publishing's list of high-quality books and multimedia programs, call 1-800-542-2595 (USA) or 1-800-461-9120 (Canada). Gareth Stevens Publishing's Fax: (414) 225-0377.
See our catalog, too, on the World Wide Web: http://gsinc.com

Library of Congress Cataloging-in-Publication Data

Ethan, Eric.
   Coral reef builders / Eric Ethan and Marie Bearanger.
     p. cm. — (Colors of the sea)
   Includes index.
   Summary: Discusses how coral reefs form, where they are located,
the different kinds, and the life found there.
    ISBN 0-8368-1737-0 (lib. bdg.)
    1. Coral reef biology—Juvenile literature. 2. Corals—Juvenile literature.
3. Coral reefs and islands—Juvenile literature. [1. Corals. 2. Coral reefs
and islands. 3. Coral reef ecology. 4. Ecology.] I. Bearanger, Marie.
II. Title. III. Series: Ethan, Eric. Colors of the sea.
QH95.8.E84   1997
578.77'89—dc2   96-47568

First published in North America in 1997 by
Gareth Stevens Publishing
1555 North RiverCenter Drive, Suite 201
Milwaukee, WI 53212 USA

This edition © 1997 by Gareth Stevens, Inc. Adapted from *Colors of the Sea* © 1992 by Elliott & Clark Publishing, Inc., Washington, D.C. Text by Owen Andrews. Photographs © 1992 by W. Gregory Brown. Additional end matter © 1997 by Gareth Stevens, Inc.

Text: Eric Ethan, Marie Bearanger
Page layout: Eric Ethan, Helene Feider
Cover design: Helene Feider
Series design: Shari Tikus

The publisher wishes to acknowledge the encouragement and support of Glen Fitzgerald.

Printed in the United States of America

1 2 3 4 5 6 7 8 9 01 00 99 98 97

TABLE OF CONTENTS

WHAT ARE CORAL REEFS?

Coral reefs consist of a substance called coral — hard limestone shells or skeletons that are made by tiny sea animals known as coral **polyps**. The limestone protects their bodies. Coral polyps are related to jellyfish and sea anemones.

Most coral polyps are very small. The body of a polyp is shaped like a tube and has a mouth at one end. Around the mouth are many small **tentacles** that have stinging cells on them. Coral polyps use these stinging cells to catch food.

There are over 2,500 different types of coral, and new types are still being discovered.

WHERE ARE CORAL REEFS FOUND?

Most coral reefs are found around the center of the Earth near the **Equator**. This is where our planet's warmest oceans are found. Coral grows best at depths of 20-60 feet (6-18 meters).

The largest coral reef in the world is the Great Barrier Reef. It is located off Australia's northeast coast. Over four hundred **species** of coral are found there.

Coral grows in many different shapes, patterns, and colors.

1. *Sarcophyton trocheliophorum*
   North Astrolabe Reef, Fiji (Pacific Ocean)

2. *Dendronephthya klunzingeri*
   Ras Umm Sid (Red Sea)

3. Mushroom coral, *Fungia fungites*
   Truk Lagoon, Caroline Islands (Pacific Ocean)

4. Gorgonian, *Melithaea squamata*
   Palau Islands (Pacific Ocean)

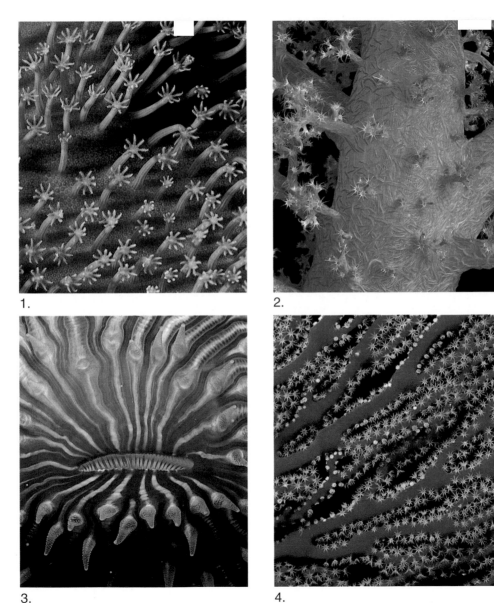

1.

2.

3.

4.

HOW DO CORAL REEFS FORM?

Coral reefs form when the limestone shells of the tiny polyps grow together and form **colonies**. When coral polyps die, other polyps build their shells on top of them. Over several centuries, large reefs form.

Most reefs are found just off shore. These are called **fringing reefs**. In the Pacific Ocean, some large reefs have grown around islands that have partially sunk. These are called **barrier reefs**. If the islands drop completely below the water, the coral reefs are then known as **atolls**. A true atoll is a coral reef that surrounds a blue lagoon. These are beautiful and rare.

The scarlet sea whip, *Ellisella*, is soft coral that has thirty to forty "whips," each 2 feet (.6 m) long.

WHAT IS PLANKTON?

Plankton is the most basic and most plentiful form of food for sea creatures in the oceans. It is made up of many different species. Most of the species are too small to be easily seen.

Crustaceans make up the most valued part of plankton. The **larval** stages of crustaceans, such as shrimp, lobsters, crabs, and water fleas, plus various types of fish eggs can be found in plankton.

The seas around these soft corals are flourishing with life.

Plankton are too small to swim against ocean currents. Instead, they drift around in large groups. Most plankton are eventually eaten by larger sea animals. But some, such as fish, crabs, and shrimp, do survive and grow to become adults.

Even though the creatures that make up plankton are very small, they are the most important form of life in the ocean. All other forms of sea life depend on plankton. If plankton were to die out, all other marine creatures would eventually die. **Pollution** in our oceans is a serious threat to plankton.

The garden eel, *Taenioconger hassi*, looks for plankton from the safety of its burrow.

HOW DOES CORAL FEED?

Coral polyps are **predators** that eat other animals, mostly plankton, to survive. Coral polyps are called **sessile** hunters. This means they gather food from a fixed position.

Most coral polyps feed at night. A polyp draws in seawater and pushes its tentacles out of its shell. Stinging cells on the tentacles stun any plankton that touches them. Small hairs on each tentacle then pull the plankton into the polyp's mouth.

The orange-cup coral, *Tubastrae aurea*, projects its tentacles into the water to find plankton.

The fairy basslet,
Gramma loreto,
hovers near coral
reefs to eat plankton.

(Inset) The arms
of crinoid coral,
Comatulida, are easily
broken, but new ones
grow in their place.

Each coral polyp is designed to help the colony of polyps find and catch the largest amount of plankton.

Sea creatures much larger than coral polyps also feed on plankton. Many species of fish, manta rays, and even whales eat plankton. The largest sea creature in the world, the blue whale, eats only plankton. Each day, it sifts tons of water through its mouth to find enough plankton to survive.

The manta ray, *Manta birostris*, even though quite large, feeds mainly on tiny plankton.

HOW DO ALGAE HELP CORAL?

Algae are simple plants that grow in water. Most coral polyps and algae called zooxanthellae help each other survive. A partnership such as theirs is an example of **symbiosis**.

The warm, clear-blue waters where coral polyps grow best do not hold much plankton. This could make it difficult for the coral to survive. But when coral do find and eat plankton, they produce by-products, such as **nitrogen** and **phosphates**, that algae need. In turn, the algae use the by-products to make sugars the coral feed on.

Dendronephthya klunzingeri is soft coral, but limestone deposits stiffen it.

Zooxanthellae cause most coral polyps to make limestone quicker than the few coral species that do not need these algae to survive.

Because algae need sunlight, zooxanthellae also limit where coral polyps can live. Zooxanthellae grow best at depths of 20-60 feet (6-18 m) and, because of darkness, cannot grow below 300 feet (90 m). In addition, algae need warm and steady temperatures. The warm ocean waters near the Equator are ideal for the partnership between algae and coral.

GLOSSARY

algae (AL-jee) — Living water plants that are food for many sea creatures.

atoll (A-tole) — A coral reef that has grown around an island that is completely under water. A true atoll surrounds a blue lagoon.

barrier reef (BARE-ih-er REEF) — A coral reef that has grown around an island that has partially sunk.

colony (KAH-lo-nee) — An area occupied by the same kind of living things.

Equator (ee-KWATE-er) — An imaginary circle around the center of Earth dividing the planet into the southern and northern halves.

fringing reef (FRINJ-ing REEF) — A coral reef that is located just off shore.

larval (LAR-vel) — The early stage of life for certain animals.

nitrogen (NYE-tro-jen) — An odorless, tasteless gas that is vital to all living things.

phosphates (FAHS-fates) — Important chemical foods for plants.

pollution (pah-LOO-shun) — The toxic wastes or poisons in the air, land, or water.

polyp (PAH-lip) — A tiny animal that lives in the water; it has a tube-shaped body, a mouth surrounded by tentacles, and a limestone shell or skeleton.

predator (PRED-a-ter) — An animal that lives by eating other animals.

sessile (SESS-ile) — Permanently attached to something.

species (SPEE-sheez) — A group of animals that are alike in certain ways.

symbiosis (sim-be-OH-sis) — The relationship between two different animals that is beneficial for both.

tentacle (TENT-a-cuhl) — Flexible, tubelike arms of a sea creature that are used for collecting food, holding, moving, or stinging.

WEB SITES

http://www.blacktop.com/coralforest/

http://planet-hawaii.com/sos/coralreef.html

PLACES TO WRITE

The Cousteau Society, Inc.
870 Greenbrier Circle, Suite 402
Chesapeake, VA 23320

Environmental Protection Agency
Oceans and Coastal Protection Division
401 M Street SW
Washington, D.C. 20460

Greenpeace (USA)
1436 U Street NW
Washington, D.C. 20009

Greenpeace (Canada)
2623 West Fourth Avenue
Vancouver, British Columbia V6K 1P8

Greenpeace Foundation
185 Spadina Avenue, Sixth Floor
Toronto, Ontario M5T 2C6

Center for Marine Conservation
1725 DeSales Street, Suite 500
Washington, D.C. 20036

National Geographic Society
17th and M Streets NW
Washington, D.C. 20036

INDEX